To you my brothers and sisters,
recovering from a painful past,
addictions, dealing with grief,
or feeling the moans and groans
of this changing world.

This message of hope is for you.

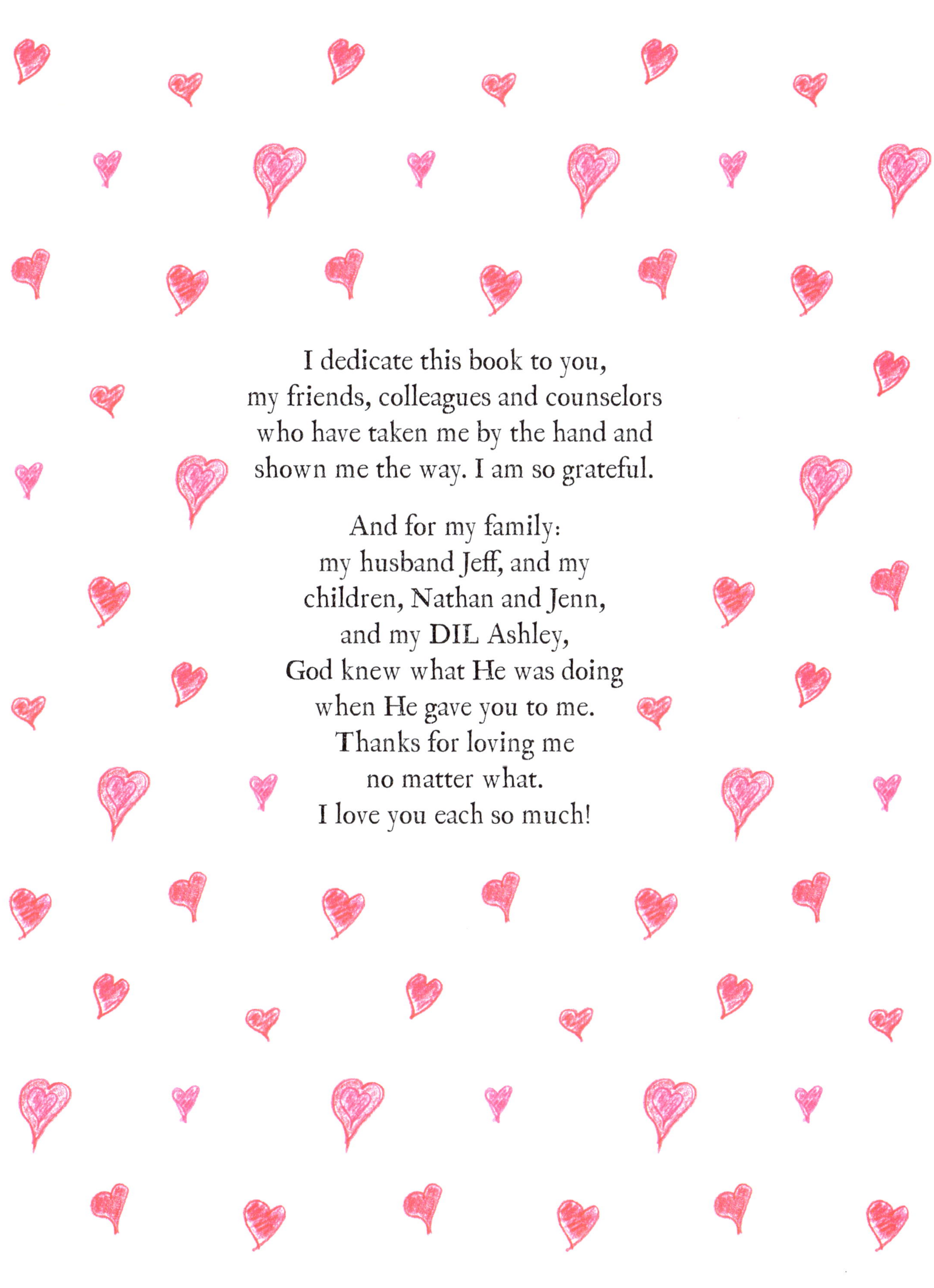

I dedicate this book to you,
my friends, colleagues and counselors
who have taken me by the hand and
shown me the way. I am so grateful.

And for my family:
my husband Jeff, and my
children, Nathan and Jenn,
and my DIL Ashley,
God knew what He was doing
when He gave you to me.
Thanks for loving me
no matter what.
I love you each so much!

Designer: Harriet Bishop
Illustrator: Debbie Kaminski

ISBN 978-1-7374628-0-4

Written and illustrated by
Debbie Kaminski

In the darkness,
before exhaustion took over,
I found a glimmer of hope.
Every night I looked up and
was awed at the majesty of
the stars that filled the night sky.
It felt like they were looking
down on me.

I believed something up there
could hear me cry and see my pain.
I prayed something bigger than me
was watching over me and
would keep me safe
through one more night.

My eyes burned in the cool wind.
I fought sleep for fear of the darkness.
And though I fought it,
sleep soon came over me.

Morning brought one more day
fighting tears and fears.
Feeling flawed and broken,
like I never belonged.
I felt like I was too much and
not enough all at the same time.
It seemed no one understood me.

I wandered on another day feeling so alone.
Another day pretending,
another day acting as if my heart wasn't tattered and broken;
another day smiling on the outside and crying on the inside.
Nobody knew my pain because I hid it.

I felt lost and alone.
So alone.

But somewhere within I found courage:
courage to push through one more day,
courage to seek a new life for myself
and those around me,
courage to heal my brokenness
so I could change the pain of
future generations.

And nighttime came once more.
Again I prayed, "Won't
someone help me find my way?
This is so hard!" I would cry
into the darkness.
"Why is it so hard?"
I shivered in the long cold nights.
I'd strayed so far from my path
I thought I'd never find my way.

I feared I was lost forever.
Some days I felt like giving up.

But then I looked up and
remembered something out
there was bigger than me.
And something was
watching over me.
And would keep me safe.
In the dark I
found faith.
And that faith
gave me hope.

Then I would whisper, "God, if you're there,
please heal me, and make this hurt stop."

Fear gripped me as the wild animals lurked in the distance.
I hoped I wouldn't fall prey to them.

I continued, “God, if there really is a God, please keep me safe through one more night.”

And again sleep would come.

As the sun rose each morning,
I was grateful I made it safely through the night.
But as I woke, those old familiar pains crept in again.
There was a gnawing in my stomach
and I felt heavy as I remembered the pain of my life.

And although the day ahead seemed so hard,
And like I was living a bad dream,
I prayed to God again.

I prayed for a better tomorrow.

I prayed for days when the sunshine
Would dance on my face
And human touch would melt my heart
and warm my body.

I prayed for freedom from
The stalking animals
And from the life all too familiar,
All too painful.

Then out of the darkness you came to me.
My Shepherd of Love.

Your Loving arms enfolded me,
Your warm body embraced me.
"You are safe," you whispered.
"You are safe, and so loved."

I felt my body
and heart warm
As you held me close.
And in the distance,
I could see the
sun's rays breaking
through the clouds.

The End

Or is it the beginning?

My Dear Brother or Sister,

You are reading this book because you are searching. Something broke you and you are searching for hope and healing. I'm so glad you're here. This book is just for you.

Your heart is broken because of abuse, fear, abandonment, or neglect, perhaps from long ago, or something recent. Perhaps you're in recovery and trying to make sense of it all. Or maybe you lost someone you love through death or divorce, or you're faced with a diagnosis that dropped you into the deepest pit of your life, and you're wondering how you'll ever get out.

I am so sorry for what you've been through and the pain that has claimed you.

You are not alone. And even though you might not believe me, you are not your pain.

I wrote this decades ago when I was in the depth of my grief from a very broken childhood.

When I was ten, my parents divorced. I remember watching my dad throw up his arms and walk away. It devastated me because I adored my daddy. I was left with an abusive step father and my passive mother, who later blamed me for the abuse. Her hurtful accusations sent me into the deepest pit of my life.

There were days when I was a pile of tears on the floor wondering why she wouldn't believe me; why she chose to believe him over me. I felt so broken and so flawed. Are you there? In a very deep pit? Wondering if there's anything on the other side? If this hurt will ever stop?

I'm here to tell you there is another side and it will stop. But you must keep the hope and keep going.

Some days I felt like my heart couldn't bear to wake up and face another day. Other days panic and anxiety took over.

But something kept calling me to cry out to God, even though I wasn't sure He existed, even though I wondered why He would let such awful things happen. And I found courage to push through one more day. Somehow I knew God was watching over me. I'd always felt Him, ever since I was a girl, crying out in the dark night in my cinder block basement bedroom. I just knew He was there.

I believe He and the angels cry along with us. As we hurt so does He, our Shepherd of Love. Those raindrops on rainy days are tears from heaven. I believe He sends angels to comfort us, help us, and get us through difficulties in life. And He'll go to any means to bring you back to Him when you're lost. Don't give up.

God sees you. He hears you. Keep going. He has a purpose for your life.

This may sound crazy, but one day He will use it to give hope to someone who needs it. I truly believe God plucked me out of my pit, set me straight, and healed my mind and my heart so I could somehow be that hope for you, right now, in your grief.

I understand grief. Some days it feels so hard to go on, doesn't it?

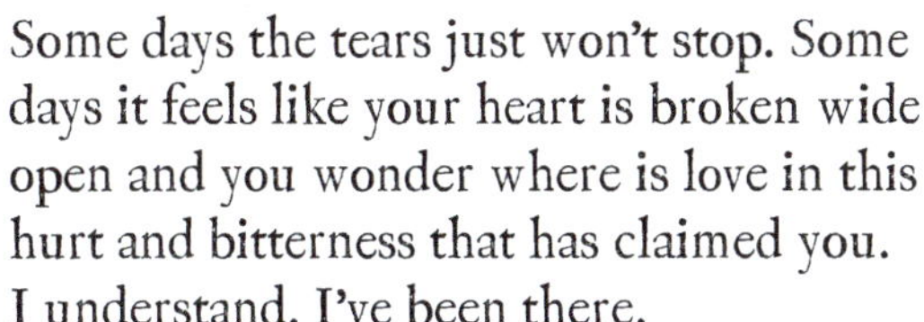

Some days the tears just won't stop. Some days it feels like your heart is broken wide open and you wonder where is love in this hurt and bitterness that has claimed you. I understand. I've been there.

Can I tell you something? You are so loved. I know that rejection, abandonment, abuse, bad news sure doesn't feel like you're loved... but you are.

Breathe in deep.
Let His love fill every cell of your being.
And breathe out your pain and grief.
Let it go. It's too much for you to carry.
And you don't have to. Let God have it.

When I realized I could give all my hurt and the overwhelming situation to God, I felt free! Trust that He's got it. It may not turn out the way you want. God never promised that. He sees you and knows what you're going through. He will take it. You just have to let it go and give it to Him.

A verse I clung to in my healing was Proverbs 3:5-6 Trust in the Lord with all your heart and lean not on your own understanding. In all your ways acknowledge Him and He will make your paths straight. Cling to his word. It's the best truth out there.

Find a trustworthy therapist, healer, mentor; someone with healthy boundaries who will love you unconditionally and help you learn to open up to love and trust again. One thing that kept me stuck was asking, "Why?" There is no hope in why. Instead, start asking, "What next?" There you will find hope.

Pause. Be silent. Listen.
The sun's rays will break through the clouds. And one day again sunshine will dance on your face and human touch will melt your heart and warm your body.

I have learned there is a huge family waiting to welcome you with open arms. You see, God showed me one day in a healing meditation that all of His children are my brothers and sisters, not necessarily the family I was born into. And the same is true for you. They are here to love you and support you. You are surrounded by a huge kingdom of brothers and sisters.

You Matter.
You Belong.
You Are So Loved.
Breathe it in.

I'm praying for you as you heal.
I'm praying for a new heart. And for you to find the shepherd who so loves you, who will leave the 99 to come and find you, and will wrap you in His arms. I'm praying for God's angels to make themselves known to you, to guide you, love you and hold you close.

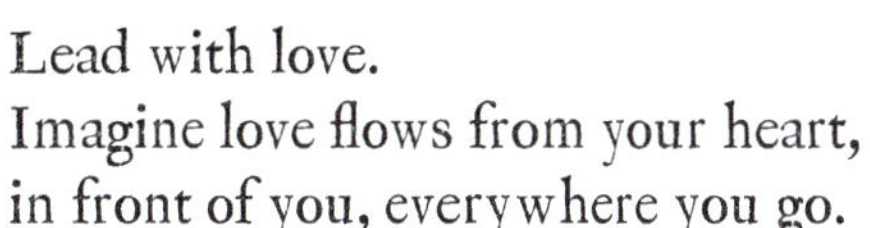

Lead with love.
Imagine love flows from your heart, in front of you, everywhere you go.

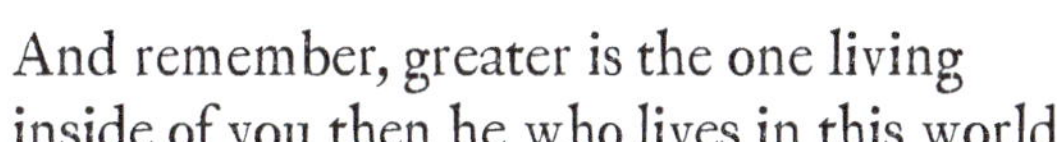

And remember, greater is the one living inside of you then he who lives in this world.

Big love and hugs to you.
You will be victorious!

Debbie

About the Author

Debbie Kaminski is the founder of *Goodbye Past, Hello Purpose* and the creator of the *Ignite Joy Project*. She's an Expert in the Mom & Daughter relationship, helping them discover the #1 secret to deep, trusting and life-long connection.

Debbie holds a master's degree in psychology and loves helping people grow through the tough stuff in life. Her clients connect both on-line and in person, in individual sessions as well as small and large groups.

Debbie is a collaborative author of the #1 International Best-Selling Book, *The One Thing Every Mom Needs to Know, Volume 2*.

She's also an expert Presenter, bringing 30+ years as a speaker and therapist to people across the globe with her signature program: *Ignite Joy – Hard stuff Hurts And Healing Happens*.

She's helped thousands of people all over the world find joy despite the hard stuff in life.

Join Debbie in this beautifully illustrated book, *My Shepherd of Love*, as she journeys with you through the darkness and into the light.

www.goodbyepast.com

goodbye past...

Hello Purpose

DEBBIE KAMINSKI

www.ingramcontent.com/pod-product-compliance
Lightning Source LLC
LaVergne TN
LVHW070225110826
845147LV00003B/645
* 9 7 8 1 7 3 7 4 6 2 8 0 4 *